Collections *for* Excellence

Assuring a Vibrant Library

Simon and Vada A. Newland
Endowment Fund
Architecture and
the Building Trades

How much House?
Thoreau, Le Corbusier and the Sustainable Cabin

Urs Peter Flueckiger

How much House?

Thoreau, Le Corbusier and the Sustainable Cabin

Birkhäuser
Basel

To Carol and Lucas, once more;
in memory of my parents Anni and Ruedi
and my brother Stephan;
and to my students.

180° Panorama, Thoreau's Cove, Walden Pond, Massachusetts
360° Panorama, Le Cabanon, Roquebrune-Cap-Martin, France
180° Panorama, Sustainable Cabin, Crowell, Texas

CONTENTS

"Simplicity, Simplicity, Simplicity!" *

* Thoreau, Henry David.
Walden; or, Life in the Woods. "Economy," p. 91.
New Jersey: Princeton University Press, 2004.
Introduction by John Updike.
Edited by J. Lyndon Shanley.

INTRODUCTION

People have been fascinated with the ideal minimal space for generations. Henry David Thoreau built a house for himself on the north shore of Walden Pond near Concord, Massachusetts, that cost a mere twenty-eight dollars and twelve and a half cents. He lived a spartan life there for two years, two months, and two days (1845–1847). During this period, Thoreau wrote the basis for *Walden; or, Life in the Woods,* a book about living simply in a natural setting through four seasons.

In 1952 Le Corbusier gave his wife Yvonne a little wood cabin, *"le Cabanon,"* as a birthday gift. The small vacation abode is in Roquebrune-Cap-Martin on the Côte d'Azur in the south of France, near the French/Italian border, the region Yvonne loved and originated from. Le Corbusier himself began to go to Roquebrune-Cap-Martin during the early 1930s on a regular basis, first as a visitor, then as a vacation guest of Jean Badovici in the villa *E.1027* that Eileen Gray and Jean Badovici had designed. After the war, he returned as a guest to Thomas Rebutato's *l'Étoile de Mer* restaurant. Le Corbusier, his wife, and Rebutato became friends and, in 1952, Le Corbusier was able to purchase his own parcel of land for *le Cabanon,* attached to the restaurant.

Thoreau's small house in Walden and Le Corbusier's *Cabanon* inspired the students at the College of Architecture, Texas Tech University, and their professor, Urs Peter Flueckiger, to design/build an ecological, economical contemporary cabin in the spirit of Thoreau and Le Corbusier.

This book explores three minimal housing solutions and their design approaches: Thoreau's house at Walden Pond, Massachusetts; Le Corbusier's *le Cabanon* in Roquebrune-Cap-Martin, France; and Texas Tech's Sustainable Cabin on the High Plains of West Texas. The book unveils some surprising similarities between the three projects through drawings and photographs. The accompanying essay, "How much House?," offers a time-critical contribution to the discourse on the ever growing size of dwellings.

Urs Peter Flueckiger,
January 2016
Lubbock, Texas

Southeast Elevation, Thoreau's House

HOW MUCH HOUSE?

In Leo Tolstoy's 1886 short story *How Much Land Does a Man Need?*, the protagonist Pahom believes that with each round of newly acquired land and wealth, he will be happier. Instead, with each round of additional acquired land and wealth, he wants more. The Bashkir people present Pahom with the ultimate challenge, for just a thousand rubles they will give him as much land as he can walk around during the course of one day, from sunrise to sunset. The only rule Pahom must follow is to be back at the starting point before the sun sets.

Pahom is thrilled at this opportunity to seize an enormous amount of land for little money. However, he miscalculates his timing. At the end of the day he runs towards the fast sinking sun. He makes it back just in time … but collapses dead from exhaustion.

His domestic buries him in an ordinary grave, thus answering the question: "How Much Land Does a Man Need?" The size of an ordinary tomb.

I remember my dad pointing me to Tolstoy's story some forty years ago when I was a child. In my imagination, I envisioned some large flat plot of land in faraway Russia. Not unlike the landscape in which I currently live, the High Plains of Texas. Growing up in rural Switzerland, to own a plot of land as Tolstoy's protagonist Pahom envisioned, was of course unimaginable. Every farmer I knew from my community could easily walk the boundaries of their farmland in a day, and many of them probably in less than an hour. I remember wondering why Pahom did not cut his route just a tad shorter? I imagined walking myself, perhaps even running for a bit, circling a part of land and then owning it—how terrific that would be. Why, I asked myself, wasn't Pahom better at managing his time and energy ... As a child my imagination felt real, I felt for Pahom. He was so close to having so much.

Americans always seem to crave larger homes. It's hard to imagine today that the average American family in 1950 lived in a home just under a 1,000 square feet. By 2007 the average home was just over 2,521[1] square feet, more than twice the size as fifty-seven years earlier. During the recent downturn of what's now known as the Great Recession, the average size of the American house dipped by a few hundred square feet. In 2013 the square foot size was trending up again averaging 2,598[2] square feet. As our single-family homes grew larger, the number of people living in a single-family household decreased. Expectations for larger spaces and more conveniences grew. A larger bedroom, with a bathroom. A bedroom for each child instead of siblings sharing a bedroom while growing up. An entertainment room, home offices for both partners, perhaps an exercise or gaming room.

In 1974 a Sony 19″ KV-1920 color television set cost $540. Adjusted for inflation, in today's dollars that would be $2,835. Very few of us would buy a TV set today with a 19″ screen. We can buy a flat-screen television more than twice that size for less than $540 in today's money. Nowadays, a desktop computer monitor or an all-in-one desktop computer is equipped with a screen as large if not larger than the Sony KV television from 1974. Not only have our homes increased steadily in square footage, we also have more possessions that we cram in them. In short, many of us just own more stuff—clothes, shoes, leisure, sports, and hobby equipment, which, when not in use, must be stored away. We have to stuff the stuff somewhere.

From the 1960s onward, a drive through a middle-class suburban neighborhood often reveals one or two cars parked in the driveway. The driveway typically leads to a double garage, which remains closed most of the time. More often than not, the garage does not accommodate the cars. Frequently its purpose is to store items we no longer need, but can't quite bring ourselves to permanently part with. Items are placed in the garage with the idea that, "Oh yes, this will come in handy someday ..." Children's toys, old furniture, seasonal equipment such as garden tools, and house decorations. Boxes of seasonal or old clothes, outdated electronics, and appliances. Sports equipment, tools, and gadgets of all kinds we once thought we couldn't do without. Over time, whether by accident or not, we transform our garages into storage facilities, a modern-day limbo. When the garage starts to burst at its seams, we hold a garage sale. The term perfectly embodies the event. We rarely sell our cars at a garage sale. Instead, we sell that stuff that we finally decided to let go for garage sale prices after an appropriate interval. Then, we can start the whole cycle all over again.

In today's information age, a never-ending, steady stream of digital data reaches us, any day of the week, at any time of the day. No matter where we might be. We have to manage e-mails, instant messages, tweets, and follow our social media updates. Many of our transactions take place digitally. For instance, we pay many of our bills online and purchase goods online. Before we order or buy anything online, the seller routinely asks the consumer for their e-mail address, and in return we will receive unsolicited e-mails promoting the vendor's latest sales.

E-mail software designers came up with the junk e-mail folder where spam and other undesired e-mails should be diverted to—an attempt to filter the steady e-mail overload of information. A co-worker at the office might casually ask, *"Did you receive my e-mail? ... ,"* of course I did, but I did not have time to respond, or I gave priority to another pressing e-mail. Or I simply forgot.

With that never-ending stream of digital data we are forced to edit and prioritize at any given time. E-mail, instant messaging, and the Internet have not only changed the way we work and communicate, but also where. Work has invaded our homes, evenings and early mornings, weekends, and vacations in the remotest locations of our planet. How many times have we told our partners, *"... wait a minute, I just need to finish this e-mail or instant message ..."* The office used to be the workplace where work was done, and home was where domestic life unfolded. Nowadays, digital work can be performed almost anytime, anywhere. Many of us use our smartphones as alarm clocks. So this device is often the last thing we see before we go to bed and the first thing we touch in the morning. The risk of information overload is obvious. The desire for a simpler life is almost natural. The cabin, the getaway home, represents not only a physical place to escape to, it represents an ideal, a metaphor in our minds where we imagine that things are clear and manageable and where we are not flooded with a digital data stream.

The recent trend of coffee-table books featuring getaway homes and cabins shows that we yearn for simpler lives. If we cannot have our own cabin, at least let's look at getaway homes in dreamy, splendid, natural settings so we can imagine how it would be if we had a vacation home. A place to relax and settle down, reflect on life and on ourselves. At a cabin, one room can be enough — a fireplace or stove spreading warmth through the space and soul. Just having some time for oneself, partner, friends, and family is important. One room appears manageable and simple — no double garage. A cabin often represents an imaginary space, a location where things become clear and manageable again because the daily routines are no longer dominated by information overload. We can all ask ourselves: How much information can a human brain process?

Henry David Thoreau — American author, poet, and naturalist — lived during the industrial revolution, a time when machine innovations were changing the manufacturing processes and the lives of the people, not unlike in today's information age. Thoreau himself was affected firsthand by the industrial revolution during his stints at his family's pencil factory, contributing to the revolution by advancing the serial pencil-making process. Thoreau, often cited as one of the first environmentalists, was also very much a man of his time, influenced by the industrial revolution. Novelist John Updike starts his introduction to the 150th anniversary edition of Thoreau's *Walden* with:

"A CENTURY and a half after its initial publication, Walden has become such a totem of the back-to-nature, preservationist, anti-business, civil-disobedience mind-set, and Thoreau so vivid a protester, so perfect a crank and hermit saint, that the book itself risks being as revered and unread as the Bible."[3]

Le Corbusier, perhaps the twentieth century's most innovative architect, and concerned with minimal living for most of his career, designed and built his *"espace minimum"* at the Côte d'Azur in France where he found solace from his Parisian daily work routine.

Both Thoreau's and Le Corbusier's minimal dwellings can fit into the double garage of an average American home today. Thoreau's house near Walden Pond measured 10′ × 15′, 150 square feet; and Le Corbusier's *Cabanon* room measures 12′ × 12′, 144 square feet. A double garage is, give or take, around 400 square feet in size, so there would be room to spare. A contemporary double garage is more spacious than Le Corbusier's and Thoreau's dwellings put together. So next time you see a double garage filled with stuff, think to yourself, "That could be a vacation dwelling."

It must be acknowledged that both Thoreau and Le Corbusier lived in their respective abodes for a limited time. Thoreau began his two years, two months, and two days living at Walden Pond in his self-built house on July 4, 1845. Le Corbusier spent his summer vacations, typically a month long, at *le Cabanon* from 1952 to 1965. Neither one lived in solitude. Le Corbusier took his meals in the attached restaurant or had the meals served in his cabin when he sought privacy. Thoreau was a self-supporter and lived off the beans he had planted and what the forest and pond held for him. Neither of them lived a hermit's life. Thoreau typically ventured once a week into nearby Concord to visit friends or take his laundry for washing. Le Corbusier and his wife enjoyed the company of the restaurant owners, the Rebutatos, and of family and friends who visited. Both Le Corbusier and Thoreau worked at their respective sanctuaries. Thoreau's *Walden; or, Life in the Woods,* which he published in 1854, would be virtually unthinkable without his years at Walden Pond. Le Corbusier made drawings from

"Objets à réaction poètique"[4] using the flotsam and jetsam that the Mediterranean Sea washed ashore and through which he scavenged for inspiration. He continued to work on his architectural projects as well. Both men took swims in their nearby pond/sea. Both had a lifelong preoccupation with minimal living, Thoreau in a more philosophically ecological way, Le Corbusier more spatially, applying and testing his Modulor measuring system on his cabin. Their respective buildings, the house on Walden Pond and *le Cabanon,* although from very different time periods, reflect their priorities.

Today's minimalism in architecture is not necessarily small or simple, rather, it's the appearance which is minimal. Often behind its minimal appearance a complex technology is hidden. Modern minimalism as a mask. Contemporary minimalist architecture is minimal in its appearance, while Thoreau's and Le Corbusier's examples are minimal in appearance but maximal in substance.

In the "Economy" chapter of *Walden,* Thoreau writes: *"... it is of a piece with constructing his own coffin, — the architecture of the grave."*[5]

Metaphorically we have completed our imaginary loop, arriving back at Tolstoy's short story *How Much Land Does a Man Need?* and its character Pahom who in the end might not even have had a coffin, the architecture of the grave, as Thoreau suggests. In the end we are all on our own individual searches of what would be our ideal sized home. How much house do we need? We are all different and have distinct answers to that question. The answer varies, too, depending on the stage of our lives, and rises and falls in our fortunes. At the end of the day, when I go to bed hoping for a refreshing night's sleep, I don't need much space. Even if I were to covet a 12′ × 12′ bed, it is not of much use once asleep. The comfort of the bed itself is what's more important during the regenerative hours of sleep. Ecologically speaking, smaller houses are more environmentally conscious than larger ones, no matter how green they are built. Global warming, manmade or not, will affect us all. Larger homes need more resources than smaller ones. Consciously thinking of how much house we need and living our life accordingly, each one of us can make an active contribution to the world we live in. As Thoreau so aptly wrote: *"What's the use of a house if you haven't got a tolerable planet to put it on."*[6]

1 Census https://www.census.gov/const/C25Ann/sftotalmedavgsqft.pdf

2 Census https://www.census.gov/construction/chars/pdf/medavgsqft.pdf

3 Thoreau, Henry David. *Walden; or, Life in the Woods.* New Jersey: Princeton University Press, 2004. Introduction by John Updike, p. ix. Edited by J. Lyndon Shanley.

4 Maak, Niklas. *Le Corbusier: The Architect on the Beach*, p. 80. Munich: Hirmer Verlag Munich, 2011.

5 Thoreau, Henry David. *Walden; or, Life in the Woods.* "Economy," p. 48. New Jersey: Princeton University Press, 2004. Introduction by John Updike. Edited by J. Lyndon Shanley.

6 Thoreau, Henry David. *Familiar Letters of Henry David Thoreau*, p. 416. Edited by F. B. Sanborn. Boston and New York: Houghton Mifflin and Company; Cambridge: The Riverside Press, 1894.

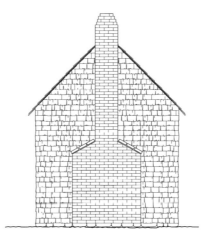

Northwest Elevation, Thoreau's House

19

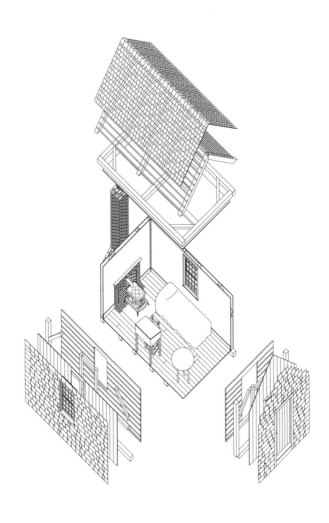

Exploded Assembly Drawing,
Thoreau's House

20

HOUSE NEAR WALDEN POND
1845–1847

Henry David Thoreau 1817–1862

From Boston's Logan International Airport it's 23.3 miles to Concord, Massachusetts, and twenty-two miles to Walden Pond. From the center of Concord to Walden Pond it's less than two miles, following Walden Street, to the original site of Henry David Thoreau's house. Thoreau went to Walden Pond from Concord on foot, often following the tracks of the Fitchburg Concord railroad which passes nearby and was built during Thoreau's time. Nowadays, most visitors arrive by car via Route 2, and turn south onto Route 126 or Walden Street towards nearby Lincoln, Massachusetts.

Thoreau's original house no longer exists. There is, however, a replica, built in the 1980s, located near the access road and between parking lots of the Walden Pond State Reservation, part of the Massachusetts Forests and Parks system. Today the location and outline of the original Thoreau house is marked by granite stones, set by self-taught historical archeologist Roland Wells Robbins and documented in his book, *Discovery at Walden*.[1] Robbins became interested in the subject after he attended the centennial celebration of Thoreau's move to Walden Pond on July 4, 1945. Several visitors to the celebration wondered where the precise location of the house was and, when no answer could be given, Robbins determined to find out. Before Robbins' findings, a cairn had emerged on the site, made by several generations of visitors paying tribute to Thoreau and Walden, and marking the approximate location where Thoreau's house had stood. But the precise position, entrance, and orientation of the house were left to the visitor's imagination.

To visit the original location of Thoreau's house, one begins at the visitor center and crosses Route 126 down to the main beach of Walden Pond, a 102-foot-deep glacial kettle-hole pond. Multiple hiking trails lead to the site but the one along the shoreline of the pond is particularly scenic. Depending on one's pace it's about a fifteen- to twenty-minute walk to the original location of Thoreau's house on an easy hiking trail.

Besides being an author, poet, philosopher, and naturalist, Thoreau was an accomplished surveyor with excellent drafting skills. While living there he made the first accurate survey of Walden Pond. Today, two dated versions of the surveys are at the Concord Free Public Library Special Collections. Both versions contain the location of the house indicated by Thoreau. One marks the house with a dot, the other version with a rectangle, giving the orientation of his house. In the chapter "The Pond in the Winter" of *Walden,* Thoreau writes: "*I surveyed it carefully, before the ice broke up, early in '46, with compass and chain and sounding line.*"[2] He goes on in detail, writing about the depth of the pond, because legend had it at the time that Walden Pond was bottomless.

In the survey drawing measuring 16″ × 21″ from 1846, he drew the rectangular outline north of Walden Pond of what's now known as Thoreau's Cove and simply wrote "*house*"[3] (page 36, 37) next to it showing the orientation and distance from the pond. The first edition of *Walden; or, Life in the Woods,* was published by Ticknor and Fields, Boston in 1854, and in it is Thoreau's 1846 survey showing the location and orientation of his house. Many contemporary Walden editions currently in print have Thoreau's survey of 1846 included as he had in its first edition. However, only the word "*house*" appears in these newer editions. The orientation and outline of the house somehow got lost.

Recent field research comparing the coordinates using a modern GPS and overlaying it with Thoreau's survey shows how accurate Thoreau's survey was. The differences between the two are marginal.

When it comes to the description of the house location, Thoreau the writer is not quite as accurate as Thoreau the surveyor. He writes in his opening of Walden: *"When I wrote the following pages, or rather the bulk of them, I lived alone, in the woods, a mile from any neighbor, in a house which I had built myself on the shore of Walden Pond Concord, Massachusetts, and earned my living by the labor of my hands only."*[4] Common understanding of *"on the shore"* would have us expect the house to be on the shore with unobstructed views of the lake. Instead, the house is north of the lakeside, some few hundred feet away from the Walden Pond shoreline. Thoreau goes on to say: *"It was a pleasant hillside where I worked, covered with pine woods, through which I looked out on the pond and a small open field in the woods where pines and hickories were springing up."*[5] That description of the site is more accurate in the location of the house. There is no known photograph of Thoreau's house while he lived at Walden Pond. The earliest one of the area dates from 1905 showing the cairn (page 29).

In the chapter on "Economy" in *Walden,* Thoreau refers to his abode at Walden Pond as a house. He does not see it as a cabin or shanty. Regardless of its small size, Thoreau applied a heavy timber-frame construction typically reserved for houses much larger in scale. Earlier in the chapter "Economy," Thoreau uses the terms, "architect," "architecture" or "architectural" several times.

"What of architectural beauty I now see, I know has gradually grown from within outward, out of the necessities and character of the indweller, who is the only builder, –out of some unconscious truthfulness, and nobleness, without ever a thought for the appearance; and whatever additional beauty of this kind is destined to be produced will be preceded by a like unconscious beauty of life."[6]

Later on in the chapter, Thoreau describes the proportion, materials and cost of his house at Walden Pond:

"I have thus a tight shingled and plastered house, ten feet wide by fifteen feet long, and eight feet posts, with a garret and a closet, a large window on each side with two trap doors, one door at the end, and a brick fireplace opposite. The exact cost of my house, paying the usual price for such materials as I used but not counting the work, all of which was done by myself, was as follows; and I give the details because very few are able to tell exactly what their houses cost, and fewer still, if any, the separate cost of the various materials which compose them:

Boards,	$ 8.03 ½	Mostly shanty boards.
Refuse shingles for roof and sides,	4.00	
Laths,	1.25	
Two second-hand windows with glass,	2.43	
One thousand old brick,	4.00	
Two casks of lime,	2.40	That was high.
Hair,	0.31	More than I needed.
Mantle-tree iron,	0.15	
Nails,	3.90	
Hinges and screws,	0.14	
Latch,	0.10	
Chalk,	0.01	
Transportation	1.40	I carried a good part on my back.
In all,	$ 28.12 ½	

These are all the materials excepting the timber, stones and sand, which I claimed by squatter's right. I have also a small wood-shed adjoining, made chiefly of the stuff which was left after building the house."[7]

It's worth noting that the land where Thoreau's house was built at the time was owned by his friend Ralph Waldo Emerson. Thoreau might have harvested *the timber, stones and sand by squatter's right,* but the timber might well be from the woodlot owned by Emerson.

After Thoreau's experimental living at Walden Pond, the house was moved back to Concord where it was used by a farmer to store grain and later dismantled. The Thoreau Institute keeps what appears to be an original partial beam or rafter among several other original Thoreau house artifacts such as bricks and handmade nails. Looking at the original pine beam one can see the ax marks that Thoreau made as he shaped it from the *"tall, arrowy white pines."*[8]

The replica of Thoreau's house gives a good sense of the space and proportions of what the original might have looked and felt like, perhaps most notable from the inside. An effort was made to use hand-hewn beams; some as Thoreau described, with the bark still on. Window boards are mounted with hand-forged nails to give authenticity to the construction method of Thoreau's time. From the outside, the roof fascia boards are machine cut and the shingles are produced by contemporary manufacturing methods, giving the replica an overly machined appearance. Perhaps most important is that the planners of the replica reproduced the house to the same orientation as Thoreau's original. So the way the sunrays and shadows travel through the window onto the furniture and the one-room space is very much as Thoreau could have experienced it more than one hundred and fifty years ago (pages 30–35). This observation inspired the photomontage of the replica onto the original site to convey a context of slope, landscape, and proximity of the pond, imagining what Thoreau saw stepping out the door. These photographs give an impression of what Thoreau's house might have looked like in its original location.

Besides the minimal dimension of the house, Thoreau was an early advocate of the reuse of building materials. Today, architects and planners reuse building materials/components to qualify for Leadership in Energy and Environmental Design points (LEED), a contemporary certification program used worldwide and initiated by the non-profit U.S. Green Building Council (USGBC), which maintains a rating system of ecological buildings and issues certificates, the highest rating being platinum.

By today's measurements, Thoreau would have received LEED points for his reuse of building materials such as the pair of second-hand windows, the old bricks, and the boards he dismantled after he bought the shanty from the Irishman James Collins.[9]

At Walden, Thoreau lived a self-sufficient life that still gives inspiration and meaning to current environmentalism. His ecological construction methods and the way he planned his house at Walden Pond are a stimulating source for architects, designers, and planners alike.

1   Robbins, Roland W. *Discovery at Walden,* 1947. Reprint, Lincoln, MA: Thoreau Society, 1999.

2   Thoreau, Henry David. *Walden; or, Life in the Woods.* "Economy," p. 285. New Jersey: Princeton University Press, 2004. Introduction by John Updike. Edited by J. Lyndon Shanley.

3   Thoreau, Henry David. Survey Drawing of Walden Pond. 133a Walden Pond [1846]. Concord, MA: The Concord Free Public Library Special Collection Programs.

4   Thoreau, Henry David. *Walden; or, Life in the Woods.* "Economy," p. 3. New Jersey: Princeton University Press, 2004. Introduction by John Updike. Edited by J. Lyndon Shanley.

5   Ibid., p. 41.

6   Ibid., p. 47.

7   Ibid., pp. 48–49.

8   Ibid., p. 40.

9   Ibid., p. 43.

Thoreau's Cove, Walden Pond, Massachusetts,
Historic Photograph 1908

Location of Thoreau's House with Cairn,
Historic Photograph from 1908

View to North, Thoreau's House, Winter

View to North, Thoreau's House, Fall

View to Northwest,
Thoreau's House, Fall

34

View out of the Southwest Window,
Thoreau's House

Ceiling Detail of Pinewood Beams,
Thoreau's House

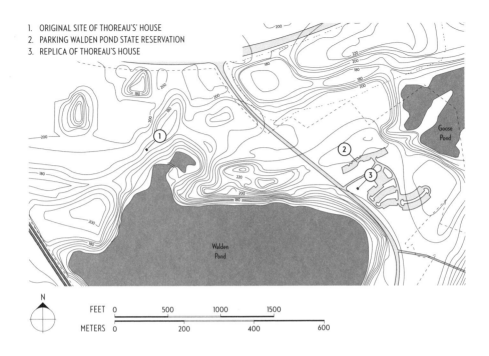

1. ORIGINAL SITE OF THOREAU'S' HOUSE
2. PARKING WALDEN POND STATE RESERVATION
3. REPLICA OF THOREAU'S HOUSE

N

FEET 0   500   1000   1500

METERS 0   200   400   600

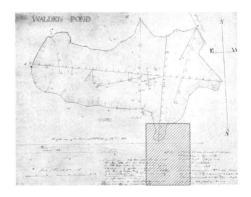

Site Plan, Walden Pond Area,
Near Concord, Massachusetts

Survey Drawing of Walden Pond,
by Henry David Thoreau

36

Detail Survey Drawing of Thoreau's House
and Orientation, by Henry David Thoreau

37

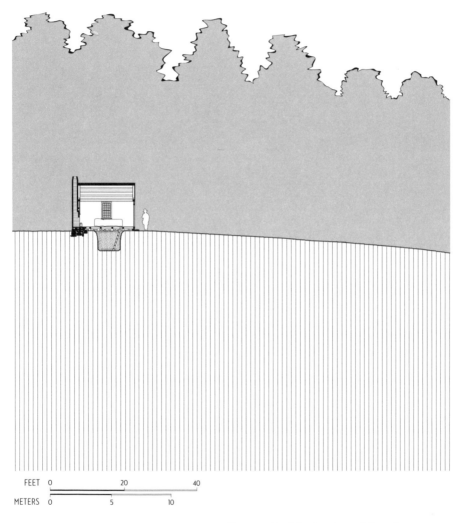

FEET   0   20   40

METERS 0   5   10

Topographical Section through Terrain,
Thoreau's House, North–South

38

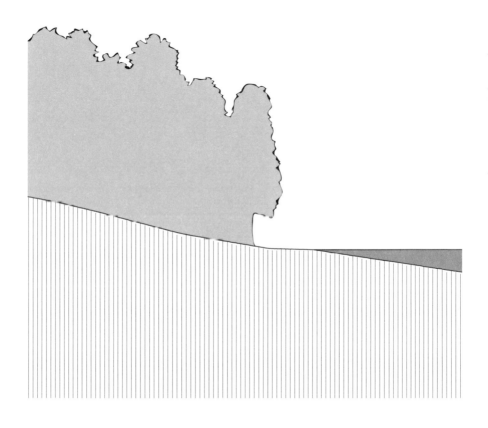

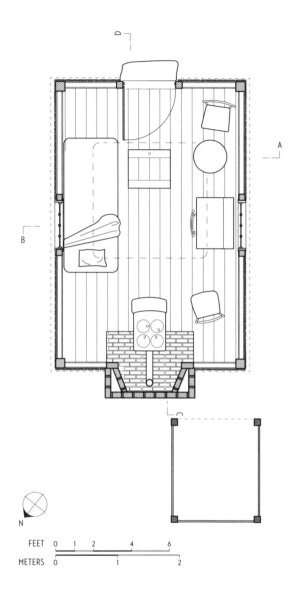

FEET 0 1 2 4 6
METERS 0 1 2

Floor Plan,
Thoreau's House

40

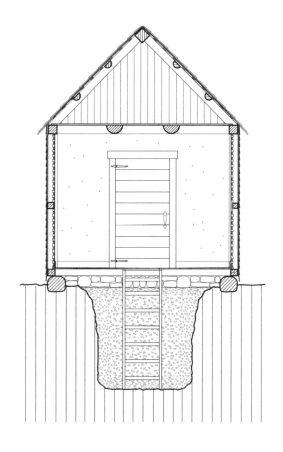

FEET 0   1   2   4   6

METERS 0   1   2

Cross Section A, looking Southeast,
Thoreau's House

41

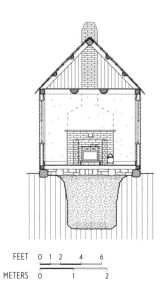

FEET 0 1 2   4   6

METERS 0   1   2

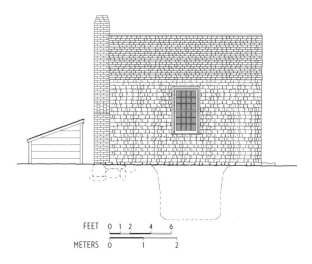

FEET 0 1 2   4   6

METERS 0   1   2

Cross Section B, looking Northwest,
Thoreau's House

Southwest Elevation,
Thoreau's House

42

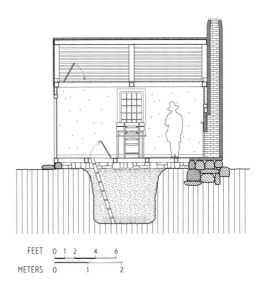

FEET 0 1 2 4 6

METERS 0 1 2

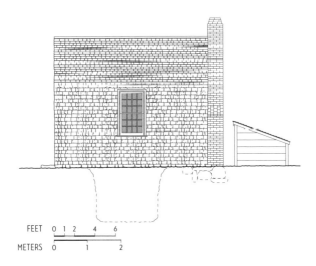

FEET 0 1 2 4 6

METERS 0 1 2

Longitudinal Section C,
looking Southwest, Thoreau's House

Northeast Elevation,
Thoreau's House

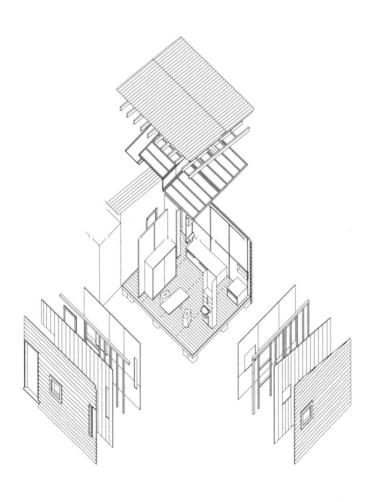

Exploded Assembly Drawing, le Cabanon

LE CABANON 1951–1952

Le Corbusier 1887–1965

Traveling by train from Nice to Roquebrune-Cap-Martin on the Côte d'Azur, one is following the same path along the French Riviera as Le Corbusier did in his time, when he embarked on a train or plane journey from Paris to Nice, continuing by train or car from Nice to Roquebrune-Cap-Martin. *Le Cabanon —* a term used for Mediterranean coastal vernacular dwellings, meaning a shed — is about ⅖ of a mile southeast of the Roquebrune-Cap-Martin train station.

Today, the station is an unmanned building, somewhat neglected, and served only by local trains. Arrivals, departures, and delays, are announced by an automated voice via audio speakers. Typically tourists visiting the area choose the more glamorous Monaco as their destination and not its *banlieues,* or suburbs.

During the summer months, two to three times a week, by appointment only, and only if the weather is good and its not raining, guided excursions to *le Cabanon* begin here. The gathering point for these tours is on the south side of the station after a walk through the passageway below the train tracks. Even though only about ten minutes by train from Monaco, it feels a very different location. No casinos or millionaires' yachts hug the shore here. Instead a public pebbled beach invites swimmers and sunbathers to soak by the Mediterranean seashore. Locals hike or run along the trail that leads all the way to the Cap-Martin, name giver of the southernmost point of the local shoreline. It's a rewarding hike with gorgeous vistas of the Mediterranean Sea and its infinite shades of blue, ranging from light aqua to a very deep, almost black, dark blue.

From the Roquebrune-Cap-Martin train station it takes about ten minutes to walk the trail, which is only four to six feet wide. (page 69). Local residents manage to squeeze motorized scooters onto the pedestrian reserved footpath. Perhaps thanks to that inaccessibility by automobiles, *le Cabanon's* location is somewhat secluded and still relatively unknown. The exceptions are the architecture enthusiasts who want to experience for themselves Le Corbusier and his wife Yvonne's favorite vacation spot or to have a glance at the Mediterranean shoreline where Le Corbusier's body was washed ashore after he took his final swim on the morning of August 27, 1965.

As is often the case with architectural destinations, it takes some effort to get here. Perhaps this is a good thing and maybe the main reason why the restaurant *l'Étoile de Mer, le Cabanon,* the *Unités de Camping,* and Eileen Gray's *E.1027* still survive. One can only imagine what an arduous task moving construction materials to the site must have been for the construction workers. As a consequence, this inaccessibility by truck or car must be translated into additional building costs from which prospective investors shied away. The footpath, mostly following the contour of the local topography with a few ups and downs, remains largely the same as during Le Corbusier's day some 70 years ago. Today, the main difference is that the surface of the footpath is no longer made of loose gravel as it was during Le Corbusier's time (page 53). The initial part of the path is now named *Promenade Le Corbusier* in honor of perhaps the twentieth century's most innovative architect. Later on, the trail's name becomes *Sentier Massolin.* The ten minutes it takes to walk from the train station to Le Corbusier's *Cabanon* allows one's mind to readjust, to create some distance, physical and mental, between one's self, everyday worries, and the stylish city of Monaco.

The silhouette of Monaco and its bay comes into view as the footpath curves slightly to the south and the shielding greenery, that private property owners planted, parts to give onto the vista. Gradually a splendid view opens over the Mediterranean Sea. The location of *le Cabanon* is situated southwest towards the Mediterranean Sea. The terraced slope gives way to the craggy rock formations near the shoreline, which merges with the lapping waves of the sea.

Le Corbusier came to know the location in the 1920s and 1930s while on vacation, visiting his wife's native town of nearby Menton. He knew about Eileen Gray's villa *E.1027* (page 68) that Gray designed with Jean Badovici from 1926 to 1929 for herself and Badovici, her partner at the time. Le Corbusier had laudatory words for Gray's villa. Later, in 1938, by invitation from Badovici, Le Corbusier and his wife spent their summer holiday at the villa *E.1027*. The following year Le Corbusier again spent time at *E.1027* and painted, without the approval and to the dismay of Gray, the murals there.

Le Corbusier returned after the war, in the late 1940s, when he met Thomas Rebutato, a retired plumber from Nice who in 1948 opened his seafood restaurant *l'Étoile de Mer,* a stone's throw away from Gray's villa. Le Corbusier asked Rebutato if he could prepare a business lunch for him and about twenty people at his restaurant. Rebutato did and it was a success. This moment marked the beginning of a lifelong friendship between Le Corbusier, his wife, the Rebutatos, and their son Robert who became an architect working for Le Corbusier.

Le Corbusier famously noted: *"On 30th December, 1951, on a table corner in a little snack bar on the Côte d 'Azur, I drew—as a birthday present for my wife—the plans for a small holiday house, or cabin, which I built in the following year on the end of a rock lapped by the waves. These plans (my own) were drawn up in three-quarters of an hour. They are final; nothing has been changed; the little house was built from a clean copy of these drawings."*[1]

He was 64 years old at the time he sketched the plans of *le Cabanon* on a table corner in Thomas Rebutato's *l'Étoile de Mer*. What sounds simple in Le Corbusier's words and is often overlooked, is that those quoted 45 minutes of design are in reality a distillate of more than 40 years of world traveling, experience in cutting-edge architecture, design, and urban planning. Le Corbusier drew on his travel experiences such as visiting Mount Athos in Greece and the Carthusian monastery of the *Certosa di Ema* outside Florence, Italy, where he admired and proclaimed the monastery cell as an ideal living quarter. All these experiences led him to plan complex urban schemes such as the *Unité d'habitation* which had elevated his standing as an architect, urbanist, and artist by the time he was 64 years old. All this knowledge could not go unheeded, and must have contributed to the design of *le Cabanon*.

Le Corbusier published *le Cabanon* on two pages in his *Œuvre Complète*, volume V, 1946–52 with the simple text stating: *"Application of the Modulor. Single room of 366 × 366 cm floor area and 226 cm height, prefabricated at Ajaccio. This type of construction has proved to be most satisfactory."*[2]

In a 1962 interview with Georges Charensol for Radio France's *L'art moderne*, Le Corbusier states: "*For my personal use I have a chateau on the Côte d'Azur that measures 3.66 × 3.66 meters. It was for my wife, it was splendid, inside was extravagantly comfortable and nice.*"[3]

In both statements Le Corbusier describes a square space, and this is not quite accurate. Somehow Le Corbusier chose to omit the corridor in that description, even though the plan published in the *Œuvre Complète* clearly shows the corridor with coat hanger system and the toilet behind it. If one includes the corridor and toilet of *le Cabanon,* the plan actually measures not 12' × 12' (3.66 × 3.66 meters), it's more like 12' × 14'-4" (3.66 × 4.36 meters).

Many scholars have written about that square space and its helicoidal geometry. The clearly zoned areas imply the sequence of a nautilus shell organizing the various zones of *le Cabanon's* living arrangement with two rest/sleep areas, a dressing area, and a work zone. In addition, Le Corbusier's implemented his Modulor, a proportioning system of measurements that he argued brought man into harmony with the built environment.

On arrival at the location, the first visible indication of Le Corbusier's building is the Modulor figure prominently painted on the facade of the *Unités de Camping* (page 56), five attached cabins that Le Corbusier designed for the restaurant owner Rebutato in 1954 and built in 1956. Proceeding further along on the trail, one can access *le Cabanon* by visiting the Rebutatos' *l'Étoile de Mer*. From the restaurant terrace, a discreet door in a screen wall allows passage onto the private patio of *le Cabanon*. Obviously, during Le Corbusier's time, access to his terrace was not for restaurant guests. Rather, the terrace was for Le Corbusier and Yvonne and perhaps their close friends, allowing them to have privacy or company when they desired. From *le Cabanon's* hallway, Le Corbusier arranged for a door to be cut so he could have access to the interior of the restaurant, its pantry and refrigerator (page 65). The door connecting the interior of *le Cabanon* to the interior of the restaurant was a clever way to avoid cluttering the spatial harmony Le Corbusier had created. Not having to bother with kitchen paraphernalia inside *le Cabanon,* by ingeniously outsourcing the more mundane tasks of daily living, kept the Modulor living pure.

If one chooses to continue walking on the trail *Sentier Massolin,* one will notice dense greenery, when the foliage gives way one overlooks first the restaurant and then *le Cabanon's* roofline with Monaco in the distance (page 61). A few steps further, at the end of the modernist complex, a chain link gate opens to a gently sloped diagonal stair leading onto the flat part of the terraced landscape. At the bottom of the stairs, near the water's edge, is Le Corbusier's *baraque de chantier* (page 60), a workroom measuring 6'-7" × 13'-2". Le Corbusier added this small studio in 1954, two years after the completion of *le Cabanon,* where he could study, write, and draw. At the end of the terrace, *le Cabanon* (page 57, 58) is attached to the Rebutatos restaurant. How one arrives will depend on the guide giving the tour that day. The latter is the one that focuses more on Le Corbusier's private universe because it gives access to *le Cabanon* without passing first through the terrace of the restaurant. The experience of the terrific view over the sea and Monaco's shoreline is rich with Mediterranean vegetation of various trees, shrubs, cacti, and the Carob tree with its enormous trunk at the center of the terrace. The tree played a vital role in shading *le Cabanon* during the hot summer months. The Carob tree's semispherical canopy easily shaded the entire *Cabanon* since a mature Carob tree can grow up to 49 feet. Today the shade of the Carob tree is somewhat diminished because the tree lost a good portion of its impressive canopy in a thunderstorm a few years ago. The historical photographs of Lucien Hervé (page 55) show Le Corbusier working outside on the terrace, the porch, a landscaped extension of *le Cabanon* and a passive cooling feature, as we would call it today. It takes one less than a minute to cross the terrace from *le Cabanon* to the *baraque de chantier*. However, the spatial experience of Mediterranean foliage and the perceptual space toward the ocean's horizon into infinity give a sensation of grandeur, and in that regard the size of *le Cabanon* is much more spacious than the self-declared 12' × 12'.

From a construction point of view, *le Cabanon* is a prefabricated timber-frame construction built and fully assembled in Ajaccio, Corsica, in the workshop of the builder Charles Barberis (page 54). Then, the prefabricated building was disassembled in parts, shipped by boat to Roquebrune-Cap-Martin and transported from the train station to its final location. The last leg of the move took place in the early hours of the morning between two and three, when the train tracks were the least used and they could stop above the location of *l'Étoile de Mer* to unload the prefabricated parts and hustle them down to the terraced location for reassembly,[4] a daunting task considering the steep slope. The interior is clad with sheets of plywood. The wooden floor is painted bright yellow and the ceiling is clad in various colored panels of green, red, white, and black. The darker colored panels are used in the rest/ sleeping area of the space. The white ones near the table/work area. The black one is exclusively used in the corridor as if the darkness of the color helps the eyes adjust to the transition coming from the outside of bright Mediterranean light to the inside or vice versa. The exterior of *le Cabanon* is clad with horizontally arranged pine wood slabs of about 4 to 8 inches wide. The slabs are nailed onto vertical wooden boards, not unlike clapboard siding seen on American houses, except that the segment-shaped cross section of the slabs give *le Cabanon* the appearance of a log cabin. Today the pine wood cladding is maintained and protected by a dark brown stain. The roof is made of two rows of corrugated fiber cement sheets cantilevering about a foot on the high and low end.

"I'm so comfortable in my cabanon that I'll probably end my days here."[5]

1   Le Corbusier. *Modulor II*, p. 239. Reimpression of the first English edition, London: Faber and Faber, 1955. Reprint, Basel: Birkhäuser Verlag, 2000.

2   Le Corbusier. *Œuvre complète 1946–1952*, Vol. V, p. 62. Zurich: W. Boesiger, 1953. Zurich: Edition Girsberger, Artemis ninth edition, 1991.

3   Cohen, Jean-Louis. Ed. *Le Corbusier Le Grand*, p. 652. London: Phaidon Press Limited, 2008.

4   Chiambretto, Bruno. *Le Corbusier à Cap-Martin*, p. 54. Marseilles: Editions Parenthèses, 1987. Ed. 2006.

5   Weber, Fox Nicholas. Le Corbuiser a Life, p. 582. New York: Alfred A. Knopf, a division of Random House, 2008.

Le Corbusier leaving Cap Martin,
next to him, Robert Rebutato

Le Cabanon assembled in the Workshop
of Charles Barberis, Ajaccio, Corsica

Le Corbuiser at work on the Terrace
outside le Cabanon

View Southwest, Unités de Camping,
seen from the Public Foot Trail

Carob Tree with le Cabanon and doorway
to the Terrace of l'Étoile de Mer

View to North, le Cabanon

View to Southwest,
between Carob Tree and le Cabanon

View to Southwest
with Baraque de Chantier

View to West,
Monaco in the Distance

View to Southwest over the Roof of le
Cabanon and partially l'Étoile de Mer

View to Southeast,
Window Detail

Window le Cabanon,
Southeast Elevation

Window Detail, le Cabanon,
Southwest Elevation

Window Handel Detail, le Cabanon,
Carob Tree in the Background

Lavatory with Southeast facing Window,
le Cabanon

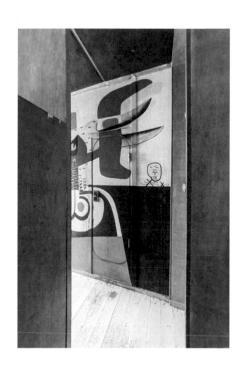

Hallway and Entrance
of le Cabanon

Mural Painting by Le Corbusier,
Hallway le Cabanon

Southwest facing Window with Mirrored
Window Shutter, le Cabanon

Southeast facing Window with Mirrored
Window Shutter, le Cabanon

Interior view or
le Cabanon

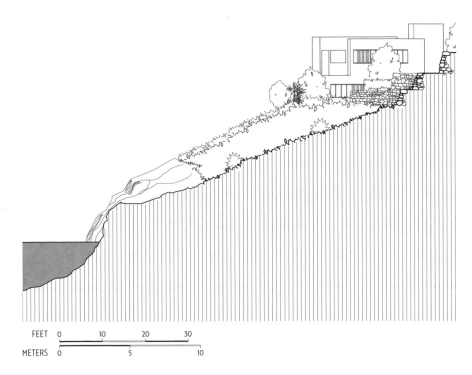

FEET 0   10   20   30

METERS 0   5   10

Topographical Section through Terrain,
E.1027,

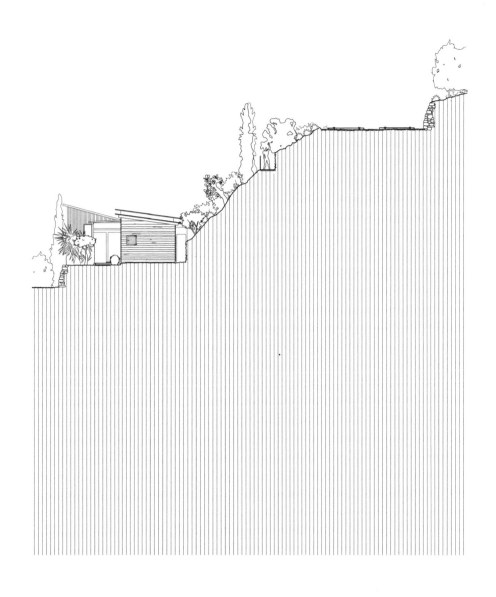

... le Cabanon, and Train Tracks,
West-East

69

1. TRAIN STATION ROQUEBRUNE-CAP-MAR
2. LE CABANON
3. GRAVE OF LE CORBUSIER AND YVONNE GALLIS

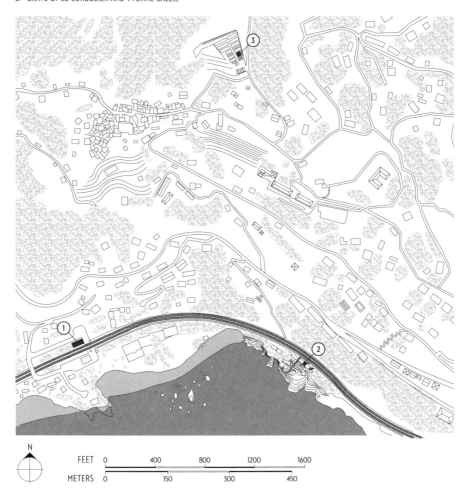

N

FEET 0   400   800   1200   1600

METERS 0   150   300   450

Site Plan, Shoreline
Roquebrune-Cap Martin

1. E.1027
2. UNITÉS DE CAMPING
3. RESTAURANT L'ÉTOILE DE MER
4. LE CABANON
5. BARAQUE DE CHANTIER

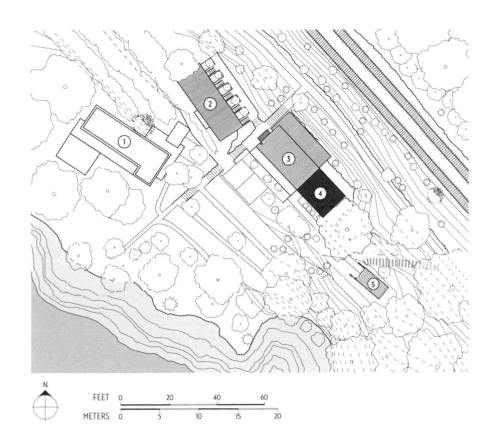

N

FEET 0   20   40   60

METERS 0   5   10   15   20

Site Plan, E.1027, Unités de Camping, l'Étoile de Mer, le Cabanon, and Baraque de Chantier

1. ENTRANCE
2. DOOR TO THE RESTAURANT L'ÉTOILE DE MER
3. CLOSET
4. ENTRANCE TO CABIN
5. BATHROOM
6. CUPBOARD
7. BED
8. LOW TABLE
9. SHELF COLUMN WITH WATER BASIN
10. TABLE
11. LOW SHELF
12. SHELF
13. WINDOW inner mirror panes on tracks and outer edge swing window (28' × 28')
14. OPENING screened w/ inner louver
    OPENING screened w/ inner louver

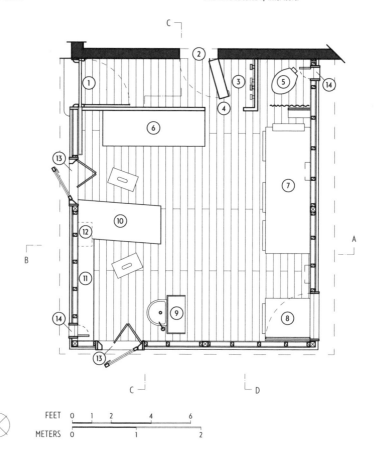

FEET 0 1 2 4 6
METERS 0 1 2

N

Plan, le Cabanon

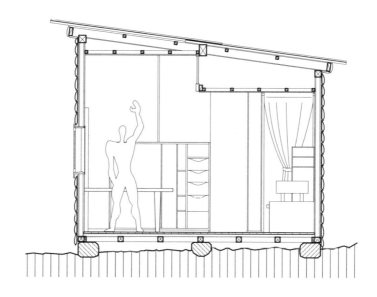

Cross Section A, looking Northwest,
le Cabanon

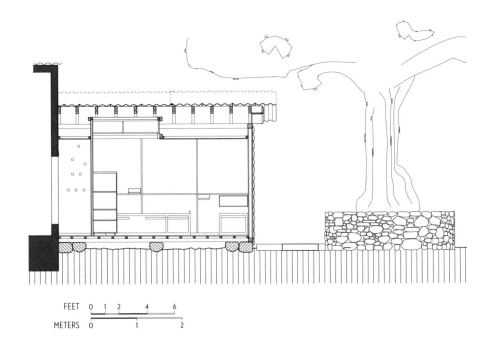

FEET 0 1 2 4 6

METERS 0 1 2

Longitudinal Section D,
with Carob Tree looking Northeast, le Cabanon

74

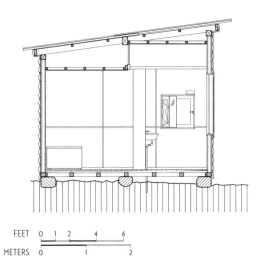

FEET 0 1 2 4 6
METERS 0 1 2

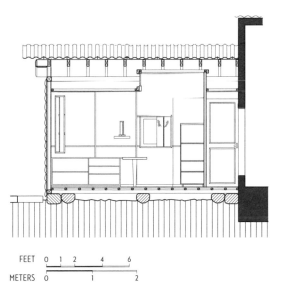

FEET 0 1 2 4 6
METERS 0 1 2

Cross Section B,
looking Southeast, le Cabanon

Longitudinal Section C,
looking Southwest, le Cabanon

75

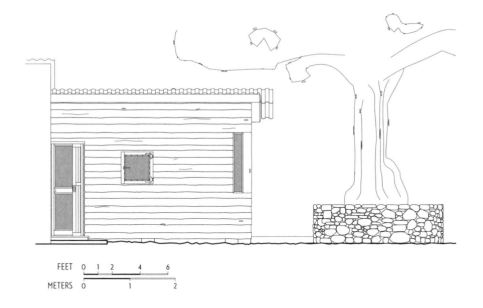

FEET   0   1   2   4   6

METERS   0   1   2

Southwest Elevation, le Cabanon

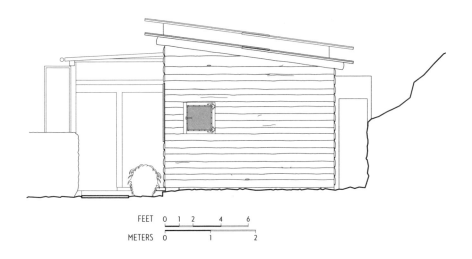

FEET 0 1 2   4   6
METERS 0   1   2

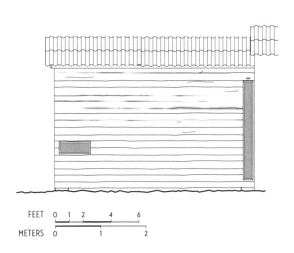

FEET 0 1 2   4   6
METERS 0   1   2

Southeast Elevation, le Cabanon   Northeast Elevation, le Cabanon

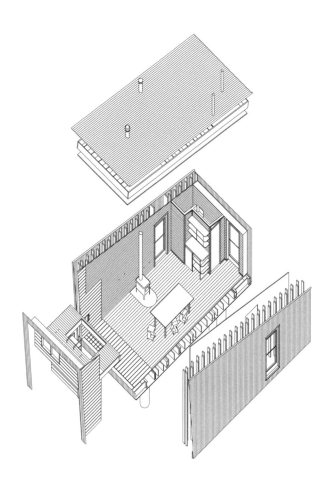

Exploded Assembly Drawing,
Sustainable Cabin

SUSTAINABLE CABIN
2008–2010

College of Architecture, Texas Tech University

Traveling west on U.S. Highway 70 past Crowell, Texas, one has to look closely in order not to miss the right turn onto farm road 1039. The farm road has no median and, after a few minutes driving on the rough asphalt, the pavement turns into a gravel road, leaving a red dust cloud behind moving vehicles. The vehicle of choice in this part of the world is a pickup truck. The truck here is not just some urban warrior toy of a hipster following the recent trend in vehicle choices. In this part of the world a truck actually has a purpose, a designated use. In rural Texas a truck is in its natural habitat, the work environment of ranchers and farmers, and a truck is their tool.

After a minute or so on the gravel road, a simple iron gate comes into view to the west and one finds oneself in a West Texas pasture, depending on the season, dry, frozen, or blooming. The Texas High Plains have a harsh wind-ridden climate with hot summers and cold winters where the temperature can change 50 degrees Fahrenheit within less than twenty-four hours. The gravel road now becomes all but a two-track dirt road with foot-long grass in the middle.

From here one can either park the truck and hike up the gentle slope of the prairie, or drive the truck to the cabin. If one chooses to continue on foot, one will see rising from the horizon the wedge-like silhouette of a tiny shiny metal building under a vast sky. The light reflection of the metal roofline and upper half facade of the corrugated iron blinks in the sun; one has arrived at the cabin.

The Sustainable Cabin is a prefabricated, ecological design/ build project by architecture, visual arts, and engineering students and faculty of Texas Tech University. The resulting research-based product is a self-contained 400 square-foot research "cabin" for a not-for-profit foundation. Begun in 2008 and completed in the summer of 2010, the Sustainable Cabin serves as an experimental research station in sustainable design and living at a remote location on the American High Plains, operating entirely off the conventional power grid, utilizing rainwater harvesting, waste composting, photovoltaic solar power, and passive solar design.

The practical need for economy forces critical inquiry into the various social and economic conditions that shape and influence contemporary design and building. The materials for Henry David Thoreau's cabin cost twenty-eight dollars and twelve and a half cents in 1845, which when adjusted for inflation to today's value would be around seven hundred and twenty-two dollars.

Admittedly, Texas Tech's Sustainable Cabin cost more than both Thoreau's house and Le Corbusier's *le Cabanon,* but all three buildings are lessons in economic and ecological design. Le Corbusier's *Cabanon* cost was 400,000 ancient French francs which translates into US$6,800 in 1952, the year *le Cabanon* was built. Adjusted for inflation that would be about $60,000 today.

The Solar Decathlon is a biennial competition held by the U.S. Department of Energy since 2002. In its first decade, collegiate design teams presented their solutions on the National Mall in America's capital Washington D.C.

The 2007 Solar Decathlon overall winner was the Technische Universität Darmstadt, Germany. While this is an excellent achievement and brings accolades to the university, it is also a high-cost endeavor in the hundreds of thousands of dollars. The logistics and costs for a prototype solar house to travel more than 1,600 miles inspired the College of Architecture at Texas Tech University to choose a different approach asking the question: How about a low-cost design/build ecological solar-powered off-the-grid building with off-the-shelf components currently available to the general public?

Conceptual sketches were drawn and grant proposals were written and historic precedents were researched. By 2008 enough funds were raised and the design/build project begun at an unheated rented warehouse on the outskirts of Lubbock. More than sixty students over a period of six semesters traded their studio tools, the computer and mouse, for a hammer and saw as part of a graduate elective course.

A comparison of a site map of Thoreau's House at Walden Pond and Le Corbusier's *Cabanon* revealed that both buildings are similarly oriented slightly tilted to the southeast. Both locations have railroad tracks passing nearby and both historical precedents have vistas over a large body of water. Both dwellings are very similar in size — Thoreau's House is 150 square feet while *le Cabanon* is 144 square feet, although the buildings are different in proportions and appearance.

In West Texas there are no naturally occurring large bodies of water unless you encounter a torrential rainstorm which, when combined with a tornado, is a force of nature no one can ignore. When the wind ripples through the high grass of the vast Texas High Plains, it looks like ocean waves curled by a moderate gale.

The Sustainable Cabin is oriented southeast, towards the town of Crowell. The cabin's exterior is clad with galvanized corrugated iron and the porch area is clad with cedar boards. The base is made of recycled steel from a defunct "double-wide." A double-wide is a form of mobile home, a contemporary American rural housing type, which is shipped on wheels, pulled by a truck in two halves, to its final destination. There, the two halves are joined together as one unit. The cabin interior is clad in white pine, and cyanotype artwork by artist Carol Flueckiger is embedded intermittently in the walls, not unlike a medieval fresco. The art is a permanent part of the whole and cannot be taken away without destroying it. The artwork makes reference to the inspirational source of the Sustainable Cabin, Thoreau and Le Corbusier. The solar photovoltaic panels are installed southwest of the cabin away from the cabin's view and behind a mesquite tree. On the northwest side, two cisterns collect rainwater with a slightly diagonally cut galvanized draining pipe. The cabin is naturally ventilated by sliding glass doors and windows. At this stage, the solar power output was not enough to supply an air-conditioning unit, but it provides enough electricity for lights, a refrigerator, and a range, plus comfortably charging the electronic devices visitors bring with them during their stay. Warmth during the colder season is provided by a modern cast-iron wood stove. Thermal insulation, a foot thick, is made out of blue denim made from cotton which was harvested on the Texas High Plains. The Sustainable Cabin's foundations are four sleeved metal tubes embedded in a concrete foundation. Once delivered to the site, the sleeved tubes with the metal-frame base of the cabin were levelled horizontally, and the top steel plates welded directly to the metal frame, soundly anchoring it to the foundation.

The dimensions of the Sustainable Cabin were determined by the reused frame of one half of the double-wide mobile home, which proportionally is two squares, each 12' × 12', making the footprint of the Sustainable Cabin twice the size of Le Corbusier's *Cabanon* room, plus the sleeping loft area. The strength of the experiment does not lie so much in the cutting-edge technology as in the testing of sustainable and solar equipment readily available to the public and applied passive heating and cooling strategies. The idea is to have a tangible example of ecological architecture for the students to see and experience, serving as a Living Research Laboratory for generations of students to come, testing the successes and shortcomings of the project and possibly upgrading its components as technology continues to develop.

Most students welcomed the hands-on experience, the change from a theoretical to a praxis-oriented making, and embraced the more haptic nature of the classwork — incorporating building materials, assembling and hoisting wood-framed walls, joining metal and wood cladding, and modifying a previously planned and drawn detail on the spot to make it buildable. These tasks, among many others in the design/build environment, let students see architecture differently, less abstract and more real. The change from analog to digital technologies in drawing and building changed the curriculum and the nature of architecture education and the profession of architecture.

The last couple of decades have revealed that academic architectural design studios have changed due to implementation of the computer and its software. Computer-aided design (CAD) and computer-aided manufacturing (CAM) methods are today's reality. The digital craft of drafting on a computer workstation has made the act of architecture representation and communication even more abstract than it was during the analog drafting days. In fact, the craft of analog drawing has lost the importance it once had. Today analog drawing is used in the conceptual stages if at all. The tactile experience of pencil or pen touching tracing paper, the individuality of the hand-drafted lines, is not the same as the two mouse clicks required to draw a line on a computer station displayed onto a monitor. Yet with all the technological advances, the Sustainable Cabin experiment has shown that students long for a haptic, tactile experience. Students want to feel the resistance of a material, the labor and sweat it takes to connect a wood stud-framed wall with the rafters of a roof. As basic and as low-tech as this may sound, an academic laboratory where fundamental construction work can be applied, explored, and tested is valuable and of merit to the students, even in our highly technological world. The design/build experience of the Sustainable Cabin hopefully will remain with the students for a long time and, when they interact on the building site with contractors and workers, give them a closer understanding of what their side of métier is. In the end that will lead to a greater understanding of the whole design/build process which will then make a better architectural creation altogether.

Texas Tech University Students raising a Framed Wooden Wall

Texas Tech University Students disassembling and recycling Materials of a Double Wide

Sustainable Cabin
leaving Lubbock for Crowell Texas

Sustainable Cabin
traveling north on Farm Road 1039

View to Northeast
Sustainable Cabin with Sunrise

87

View to Northeast, Sustainable Cabin
with Solar Voltaic Panels and Water Tanks

View to Southeast, Sustainable Cabin
with Thunderstorm Clouds

View to Northeast, Sustainable Cabin

View to Northwest, Sustainable Cabin

91

View to Northwest,
Sustainable Cabin, Porch

View to East,
Sustainable Cabin, Porch Detail

93

View to East, Sustainable Cabin

View to Southwest, Sustainable Cabin,
Detail Bathroom Window and Water Tanks

View Interior with Table and Stools,
Sustainable Cabin

View Interior with Table and Stools,
Sustainable Cabin

View Interior, Sustainable Cabin,
Sliding Door to Porch

Sustainable Cabin, Coat Hangers with
Cyanotype Artwork by Carol Flueckiger

Sustainable Cabin,
Cyanotype Artwork by Carol Flueckiger

1. SITE SUSTAINABLE CABIN   3. US HIGHWAY 70
2. FARM ROAD 1039   4. TOWN GRID OF CROWELL, TEXAS

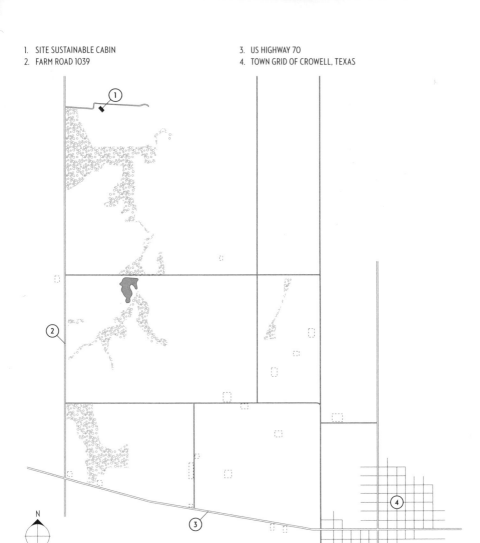

N

FEET   0   2000   4000   6000

METERS 0   500   1000   1500   2000

Site Plan of the Town Grid and Cabin
Site of Crowell, Texas, and Area

100

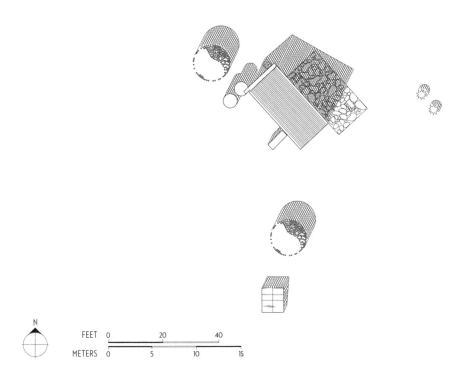

FEET 0   20   40

METERS 0   5   10   15

Site Plan, Sustainable Cabin, Patio, Water Tanks,
Solar Voltaic Panels, and Mesquite Trees

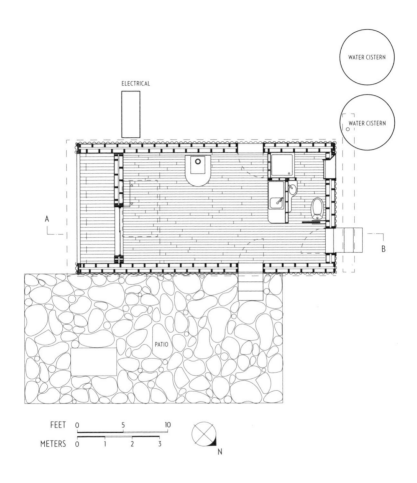

WATER CISTERN

ELECTRICAL

WATER CISTERN

A

B

PATIO

FEET 0   5   10

METERS 0   1   2   3

N

Plan, Sustainable Cabin

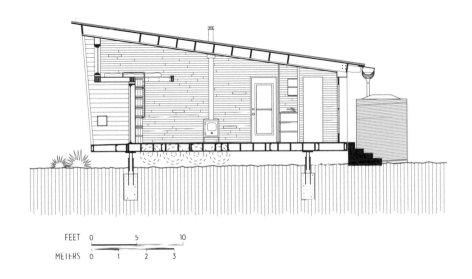

FEET 0   5   10

METERS 0   1   2   3

Longitudinal Section A,
looking Southwest, Sustainable Cabin

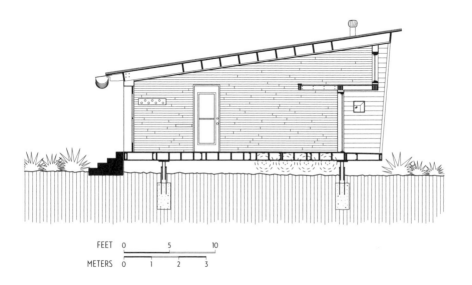

FEET 0   5   10

METERS 0   1   2   3

Longitudinal Section B, looking Northeast,
Sustainable Cabin

104

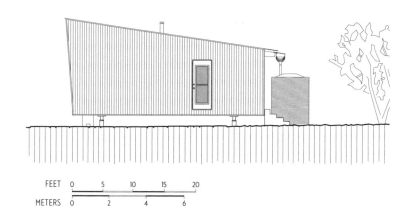

FEET   0   5   10   15   20

METERS   0   2   4   6

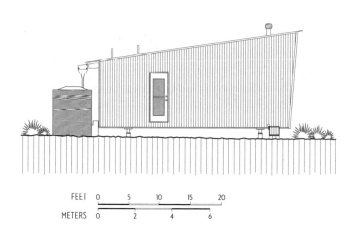

FEET   0   5   10   15   20

METERS   0   2   4   6

Northeast Elevation,
Sustainable Cabin

Southwest Elevation,
Sustainable Cabin

105

Texas Tech University Students at Campfire
with Sustainable Cabin

Sustainable Cabin at Dusk

ACKNOWLEDGMENTS

This book, like a work of architecture, is both an individual and a collective undertaking. Without the support and help of the people and organizations listed below, the book would not have been possible.

I am grateful to the Texas Tech University Office of the Vice President of Research Scholarship Catalyst Program, and TTU Faculty in the Creative Arts, Humanities and Social Sciences Competition, which recognized the importance of this book and made it possible though their generous support.

Special thanks are due to Arnaud Dercelles, Bénédicte Gandini, Michel Richard, and Delphine Studer of the Le Corbusier Foundation and to Jeffery S. Cramer of the Thoreau Institute. All of you took time answering questions and letting me have access to your respective archives.

I thank historian Richard Smith for the thoughtful tour of Walden at Walden Pond and his insights into Thoreau's time and life.

I am grateful to Stephanie Bunt, Texas Tech, College of Architecture graduate, who over countless hours did the drawings specifically drawn for this book.

I am in debt to Denny Mingus for the photo-editing and the composition of the photomontage of Thoreau's House and the stitching of the panoramas.

A special thanks to Clifton Ellis, who never tired of reading and editing my writing from my hybrid language of Swinglish (Swiss/English).

I thank Annette Gref and Katharina Kulke from Birkhäuser Basel, for the coordination and oversight of the book, and Julia Dawson for the copy editing. Thomas Neeser and Thomas Müller from Neeser & Müller for their keen eye when designing this book.

There are a number of people I am grateful to have known and worked with. They generously gave their time to talk to me and help me, each with their own specific expertise. I thank Kevin Brown, Hendrika Buelinckx, Robert V. Duncan, Taylor Eighmy, W. Mark Gunderson, Saif Haq, Christopher R. Hidalgo, Glenn Hill, Kathy Johnson, Michael A. Jones, Michael Martin, Paola Pellandini, Bob Perl, Bonnie Reed, Michael San Francisco, Ben Shacklette, Henry K. Sharp, Gary Smith, Andrew Vernooy, and John White.

Last but not least, a heartfelt thank you goes to my family, Carol and Lucas, to whom I dedicate this book.

CREDITS AND NOTES

Photographs

All photographs are taken by the author unless otherwise noted.

p. 5: Panorama Photos by the author, photo-stitching by Denny Mingus

p. 28: Detroit Publishing Company, Library of Congress. Please see Details: http://www.loc.gov/pictures/item/det1994020348/PP/

p. 29: Detroit Publishing Company, Library of Congress. Please see Details: http://www.loc.gov/pictures/item/det1994020349/PP/

pp. 30–35: Photo by the Author, photomontage by Denny Mingus

pp. 36–37: 133a Walden Pond Survey, Drawing by Henry David Thoreau, 1846. The Concord Free Public Library, Special Collections, Henry David Thoreau's Land and Property Survey's.

p. 53: Photographer unknown. Scanned from the book: Le Corbusier, Edited by Willy Boesiger, Verlag für Architektur, Artemis Zürich 1972, p. 96. Same Photography is also published in: Eileen Gray L'Étoile de Mer Le Corbusier, Trois aventures en Mediterranee archibooks Paris. 2013. P. 80. Credit is given to: Le Corbuiser quittant Cap-Martin suivi de Robert Rebutato © F.L.C. / ADAGP, Paris 2013

p. 54: Photograph from the François Barberis Collection, Montpellier. Scanned from Le Corbusier – The Measures of Man, Edited by Olivier Cinqualbre and Frédéric Migayrou. Scheidegger and Spiess, 2015. p. 215.

p. 55: Photographer: Hervé, Lucien.

pp. 86/89/91/92: Photographer: Mingus, Denny.

Drawings

All drawings are drawn by Stephanie Bunt in collaboration with the author unless otherwise noted.

Credits Sustainable Cabin

Participating Students, Texas Tech University

Spring 2008: Deborah Bradshaw, Justin Mecklin

Summer 2008: Piotr Chicinski, Michael Driskill, Cory Folsom, Brandon Pryor

Fall 2008: Joshua Atkins, Sara Bradshaw, Nicholas Genzer, Amanda Glidewell, Ginger Kapalka, Sergio Lainez, Jenna Murphy, Jordan Mussett, Eric Ritchie, Chelsea Sekula, Daniel Takahashi, Douglas Zimmerman

Spring 2009: Cody Carriker, Michael Cast, Sean Cox, Joseph Engelhardt, Edgar Gallegos, Amanda Glidewell, Mckee Kelly, Ryan Kimberling, Lindsay Kunz, Bradley Latson, Aaron Marshall, Wesley McElhany, Kyle Meason, Kyle Robertson, John Simons, Warren Toups

Summer 2009: Ian Britt, Stephanie Hanlon, Cherese Wheeler

Fall 2009: Donovan Blakeley, Taylor Coleman, Crystal Davis, William Denman, Edmundo Fortuna, Justin Hackleman, Alex Kneer, Tyler Marks, Kory Murphy, Jonathan Pace, Lauren Rentschler, Kenneth Roberts, Andrew Stiglmeier, Andrew Tyler

Spring 2010: Gregory Hemmelgarn, Brendon Hoffman, Jonathan Lemaster, Christina Liebelt, Gilberto Lopez, Phillip Miller, Michael Morow, Kenneth Olson, Garik Rowe, Parker Sands, Amador Saucedo, Brian Wills, Austin Wilson

Fall 2010: William Cotton, Ji Eom, Jason Fancher, Michael Franks, Joshua Krantz

Faculty from the following Colleges and Departments

College of Architecture: Urs Peter Flueckiger, Dipl. Arch. SIA, Professor, Michael Martin, Architect, Instructor, Ben Shacklette, AIA, Assoc. Professor

College of Visual and Performing Arts, School of Art: William Cannings, Assoc. Professor, Carol Flueckiger, Assoc. Professor

College of Engineering, Department of Mechanical Engineering: Derrick Tate, Assistant Professor

Texas Tech Staff Members: Sam Beavers, Mark Bond, Denny Mingus, Fred Porteous, Julie Rex

Individual and Company Sponsorship: Texas Tech University Research Enrichment Fund Grant. Fred Koch, Stacy Henry, and Jon Black, The Pease River Foundation, Crowell, TX, F. Marie Hall, Midland, TX, John Dea, Dea Door and Window Co. Lubbock, TX, Mike Harendt, MBCI Metal Buildings, Houston, TX, Rex Neitsch, Thermal Insulation, EcoBlue, Lubbock, TX, Larry Harvey AIA, Chapman Harvey Architects, Lubbock, TX, Lumber Liquidator, Flooring Systems, Amarillo, TX, Craig Shankster, Energy Efficient Wood Stoves, Morsø USA, Portland, TN, BioLet, Toilet Systems, Fresno, OH, Lowe's Home Improvement Center, Lubbock, TX, Encenex Corporation, Roof Vent Systems, Sugarland, TX, Cris Been, Therma Breeze, Solar Solutions, Lubbock, TX

About the Author

Urs Peter Flueckiger practices architecture in Lubbock, Texas, and teaches at Texas Tech University where he is a Professor of Architecture. He worked for several architecture firms in Switzerland including the office of Mario Botta. He worked in the office of David Rockwell in New York City before joining the faculty at Texas Tech in 1998. He holds a Master of Architecture degree from Virginia Polytechnic Institute and State University Blacksburg, Virginia. His design and research interests include economical ecological housing, minimalism in architecture, design/build process, and modernism of the 20th century to the present-day. In 2004, he and his wife Carol designed and built their current house and studio based on Flueckiger's design philosophy. His design work has been published in "The New York Times," "Texas Architect Magazine," several books, and numerous periodicals. He is the author of the book Donald Judd, Architecture in Marfa Texas. When he is not thinking about architecture or having fun with his family, he loves riding classic BMW "airhead" motorcycles across the High Plains of West Texas.

Urs Peter Flueckiger

How much House?
Thoreau, Le Corbusier and the Sustainable Cabin

Copy editing: Julia Dawson
Project management: Annette Gref, Katharina Kulke
Production: Katja Jaeger
Layout, cover design and typesetting: Neeser & Müller GmbH, visuelle Gestaltung, Basel
Typeface: Media 77 by André Gürtler, Christian Mengelt & Erich Gschwind
Paper: 130g/m² Schleipen Fly weiß
Printing and Binding: DZA Druckerei zu Altenburg GmbH, Altenburg

Library of Congress Cataloging-in-Publication data
A CIP catalog record for this book has been applied for at the Library of Congress.

Bibliographic information published by the German National Library
The German National Library lists this publication in the Deutsche Nationalbibliografie;
detailed bibliographic data are available on the Internet at http://dnb.dnb.de.

This publication is also available in a German language edition (ISBN 978-3-0356-1026-0)
and French language edition (978-3-0356-1029-1).

© 2016 Birkhäuser Verlag GmbH, Basel
P.O. Box 44, 4009 Basel, Switzerland
Part of Walter de Gruyter GmbH, Berlin/Boston

Printed on acid-free paper produced from chlorine-free pulp. TCF ∞

Printed in Germany

ISBN 978-3-0356-1028-4

9 8 7 6 5 4 3 2 1

www.birkhauser.com